Tongue

Tongue

poems by

RACHEL CONTRENI FLYNN

Red Hen Press | *Pasadena, CA*

Tongue
Copyright © 2010 by Rachel Contreni Flynn
All rights reserved

Book design by Mark E. Cull
Book layout by Sydney Nichols

Library of Congress Cataloging-in-Publication Data

Flynn, Rachel Contreni.
  Tongue : poems / by Rachel Contreni Flynn. — 1st ed.
    p. cm.
  ISBN 978-1-59709-475-7
  I. Title.
  PS3606.L937T66 2010
  811'.6—dc22
                            2010007173

The Annenberg Foundation, the James Irvine Foundation, the Los Angeles County Arts
Commission, and the National Endowment for the Arts partially support Red Hen Press.

First Edition

Published by Red Hen Press
Pasadena, CA
www.redhen.org

ACKNOWLEDGMENTS

Grateful acknowledgment is made to the editors of the following publications for first publishing these poems, a few in earlier versions: *Bellevue Literary Review*, "Saint Elizabeth"; *jubilat*, "Small Gray House"; *Southern Indiana Review*, "Gemstones"; *Sou'wester*, "Slice of Glass"; *The Same*, "Hunger for Something Easier"; and *Whiskey Island Magazine*, "Indelible."

Thanks to the National Endowment for the Arts and Michael Flynn who gave time, space, and support to complete this book. Special thanks also to Red Hen Press, Eloise Klein Healy, Katharine Wardlaw, Stephanie Slatkin, and Mary Jane Nealon for believing in this work and in me.

I am most grateful to Patrick Flynn and our children—

> . . . a shoreline of sweet light inside my chest
> so that my soul could sail.
> —Rafael Alberti, *The Good Angel*

The first line of "My Anxious Whisper is a Form of Fierce Sweetness" is Plutarch's.

For Judith

Contents

HOLLOW

Gnaw

ANOTHER MIRROR

A sister! Another mirror!
—Boris Pasternak, *Sister-Life*

Warm ocean. Tight.
              Low sounds
and always the thud

of a modest slipper above:
              step shuffle . . .
step shuffle.

Wet cave. Murky shadows.
              Glisten
and shift.

When my eyes open at last, I spend weeks
growing immense, squinting at the drawings
left on the walls by the first girl:

stick figures in all postures of play and prayer,
escape and disguise. Then emerging, the words
I will learn to read later in everything she does:

    I am waiting for you

              to hate and to love.

Sand in the Gas Tank

We were allowed to go everywhere. We were allowed, and therefore

we ransacked the Cozy Camper parked behind the hardware store, stole change and tiny bottles of rum then shoved handfuls of sand in the gas tank.

We drank the rum and got sick in Moots Creek.

We swam in the creek, and leeches sucked on our legs. Bobby Justice burned them off with a cigarette.

We smoked cigarettes in an abandoned bomb shelter full of girlie mags and canned beans.

We leafed through the girlie mags and felt fat, ugly, flat.

We planned to run away, biking along the highway, until the semis scared us into a culvert.

We met in the culvert a great blue heron that bolted up, also scaring us.

We were alone with each other.

We loved each other in the dirt and sweat and hardship we imagined constructed us.

We were allowed to construct a story around the small town that sheltered us. We were never alone. Always the widow in the upstairs window squinting as we sloshed in Moots Pond. Always the farmer noting the heron. Always each other.

If there's sand in the gas tank, we put it there. If we've revved and sputtered and forgotten ourselves, we should be ashamed. Once we were sisters, dirty and scared, but pedaling.

  Allowed to go everywhere.

Gnaw

So many photos:

the pretty tow-head with her fist
twisted in her mouth, gnawing.

Our mother shellacked my sister's nails
with noxious liquid and begged.

But it was like a weed-tree growing
alongside a fence, helpless,

striving for light and release
finding instead the bite

of metal bending, imbedding
in pulpy green flesh.

The tree and the fence, both
damaged, neither happy.

CLOAK

The nook under the stairs,
full of books. Once

my mother spoke in there,
softly. Outside the door

I waited, not yet
crying. She curled

on the floor in a rough cloak,
locked with the phone

in an awful cottage,
cajoling

the woodsman to come
chop it down.

Gemstones

We believed that kernels of seed corn scattered
in the fields and covered with dusty fertilizer

were gemstones—citrine and opal, peridot.
We made necklaces of them. No one told us

we were beautiful. No one told us
we wore poison around our necks.

🌀

We also stole
from the drugstore's
Honor Bowl.

We filled
paper cups with cream
and fake sugar

and drank
at the Formica table
with ancient farmers waiting

for sacks of pills.
One sister
twirled and sang,

a goldfinch, a cricket,
while the other
busied herself

at the Sanka can
up front, stuffing
nickels in her pockets.

We took more money from our drowsing father, bought a platter of fried shrimp
at the Top Notch Grill, then swung our plump legs from the vinyl stools.
Two faces, the same, with different hair.   Our bodies took it in,

the flesh and grease and batter, the guilty lunch. We were becoming
what became essential: history and hunger, a startled kind of anger.   Along the counter
we arranged the change into a freight train—box cars on stately, silver wheels.

Years later we are unhappy
in the useless way

a slice of soap parches
at the edge of the utility sink.

A little perfume, mostly quiet.

One summer an odor like the underside
of everything bulged from the woods,

and we found a young cow, its forelegs tangled
in the wire fence, dead and swollen at the lip
of the field. Funny how it stayed that way,

worsening in its sameness. Funny how it starved
then filled up so magnificently on air and time.

DEEP

There's a blade
in the hay mow

and we're jumping.

Saint Elizabeth

1.

A scarecrow came for breakfast, sat in my sister's seat and refused
to eat. It combed its straw hair with shredded hands, fluffed its
limbs and made chit-chat, happy faces, horrid little predictions.

2.

She was blonde and tough
and flawless in her
flute-playing. I thought

she played to wake me
on winter mornings,
the sweet gavotte.

I was wrong. She despised
the dark animal of me,
my dirt-scent, my clawing,

my knotted hair. But the flute
told its falsehoods, then she left
as a ghost: coldly, lightly

as the gavotte, as birdshot.
And me, a possum caught
in the yard at dawn.

3.

My sister left for a few weeks, and the lid lifted
off the stock pot. The house filled with the possibility
of eating bread dunked in the savory thickness

of her absence. I was happy. Happy to sit
in the kitchen, thinking. Happy to carry
the baby—a sack of sweet apples against me.
She was gone, and I was glad the steel edge
of her had stopped carving all the faces
in the house into shriveling dolls, gouging eyes
out of the simple starch of us.

4.

Even the hospital bore her name, called her Saint.

I too was sick. Of driving and sitting. Of nodding.

I knew the big building that held her would not heal her.

At home I gathered mulberries in the woods.

I told my brother stories in the barn that began

Once there was a bag of sadness locked in the attic.

5.

Because she harms herself

we're scared into applause, and because she steals everything shiny,
a frantic magpie, we creep behind her: silent butlers returning the lighters,
the cufflinks, the neighbors' spoons and coins.

Because she forbids us

to forbid her the liquor cabinet, the car crashes, we pray she'll go away
like a bit of milkweed silk. Instead she returns, a dog in pain no one

will put down, that stains the carpets and wakes us all night with sharp barks
until someone rises to let her out, knowing she won't go,

and she won't.

6.

The girl lies small, pale, naked in bright sunlight
across a tightly made bed. She ages before my eyes—
bones rise up, legs lengthen, but no hair anywhere
except the hay-lightness around her head which turns
and her mouth, the only red in the room, begins to scream.
This is my sister, it seems. I close the door and back away.

7.

Even in dreams
I back away.
I forsake her.
I laugh and run.

It is too much. The brightness of her,
and the love. I understand certain things

about religion. How it is to continue
to believe in the implausible thing.

As a child, I only wanted my sister's body
against me in sleep. Even now I dream

of her breath in my hair. I wake feeling
saved, then bitten and torn down.

GIFT

Summer day
soft lovely
two sisters

romping
in the graveyard
pulling

fresh flowers
from headstones
and running

home giving
the bunch
to our mother

who cried
she was so
happy

we'd bought her
a gift and her
happiness has left

a smudge
on the innermost
of my chest.

Tongue

In her twelfth summer, a girl left the Midwest for an island in Maine where her brilliant, ill grandmother lived in a cottage on a pine-rimmed lake. The girl was to keep house, to keep the old lady company. Back home, her older sister starved herself. That summer, the island was troubled by the discovery of a human tongue on the beach.

ARRIVAL

The girl walks the rutted drive
with her suitcase and radio.
              She is mostly
              eyes and hair,
              and the shadows flare,

then retreat around her.
What's before her stacks up
at the end of the path:
              low house
              wide lake
              mountains.

She believes she will lie
in a hammock for weeks, reading.
              A bowl of nectarines.
              Dragonflies.
              Sleep.

STORY

1.

What she thinks, she thinks alone. Therefore
she unpacks her little girl treasures into the bureau,
twists her hair into a long braid and goes out to walk
in the light and dark woods. She waits on a gray rock
for the story to start: wilderness, mystery, magic.

What else is there?

2.

She sleeps in a small room
under a red coverlet. The lamp

casts cozy shadows. At 2 a.m. she's called
to rise, to hoist her Grandmother

to the toilet. Most nights
the girl must wipe. She protects

her nightshirt by placing her palm
between the wobbly thighs.

She protects herself by making fiction
of what's happening. *This is a goat*

overstuffed with milk, the liquid flowing
down its helpless gray teats.

In the morning, the goat insists
on toast spread with anise butter

and eggs Benedict. *I am serving
a heart-broken queen in a remote castle.*

*I am serving a just-freed prisoner of war,
a sentence for my lover's theft, or else penance.*

3.

Back home her friends prepare for the County Fair. Who to ride with on The Zipper?
How to trick the parents into ignorance, to pick them up late? The girl would like
to wander around almost sick from The Zipper, sucking a Slushie, giggling at the
ruminants—the giant genitals!—pissing in their pens.

4.

Her vague, pot-smoking aunt drops her
in Bar Harbor, and the girl follows
a solid woman into a small card shop,
loiters close enough to smell Avon,

to brush against the soft edges
of the appliquéd sweatshirt until
the actual daughter bursts in clutching
a pop-eyed velvet lobster and swings,

contented, from her mother's sensible purse.

5.

The story will be finished

                              in five weeks' time.
Not nearly a semester.

                              Not long enough to need a haircut.

In 7th grade, the girl read *Beowulf.*

                    She loved the arm hanging in the banquet hall,

all the rough, bloody ugliness of it.

                    She loved the rise from the primordial swamp,

the mother's rage.

The girl forages in the mud out back

                    for salad fixings,

still imagining

                    she's Gretel, Rose Red, Rapunzel,

that she must untangle

                    the muck, dismay, disgust

and force the story

                    to its rightful

unfolding:

                    freedom, true love.

What else is there?

6.

One afternoon, the sun eclipses. The girl

places her hand to her eyes, risks blindness
by peeking through. What she sees
is a bitten English muffin, and she's been tricked.

No father dashing, repentant, along the path
to gather her up. No pale sister holding her hand.
And no sturdy brother shoving the hag

into the oven's maw. No hammock, no nectarines.
She'd thought when the sky ate itself, she'd drop
to her knees on the dock, drop the flabby radishes,

and be changed.

LOVE

The Grandmother's arms. Bruised, slack. Ending in garlic bulbs, yellow and smoking. Always the smoke and the crystal goblet. The girl knows these arms held her own mother. And let her go.

ENEMY

Enemy made flesh and fur,
the coon cat Griselda skulks
from the cellar—consort
of the axe and turpentine.
The girl need not imagine evil,
it sidles up to her: enormous,
shit-eyed and blood-toothed.
Hatred leaps and seethes.
Fur clots. The girl locks
Griselda in the garage
every chance she gets.

LUPINES

She learns
to perform her tasks
promptly, to adopt

a blank face.
Then to the forest:

soft moss, Jack-in-the-pulpit,
goldfinches, water-slick rocks.

She learns the fragility
of lupines—the magnificent

purple yearning upwards—
that once picked flop grayly,

dead rats in a basket.

She learns to go away
and do awful work
in a lovely place.

THE WORK

To polish. Tiny collector's spoons. One: a miniature devil perches, cross-legged and laughing.

To scrub. Everywhere. Floor/baseboards. Sink/faucets. Goblet/lipstick. Toilet/vomit.

To peel and shuck. Potatoes and corn. On the dock, the girl sits with a bushel basket talking to her sister's hair—just this color, just this falling out and away.

To cut. Ovals in sheets and wool blankets. Snip away the scorch marks, leave empty spots. Burned bits pile up in her lap. The linens here look like a child's worst idea of ghosts.

To cut. Burrs from cat fur. The girl's face fills with dander and flecks of dirt, dried chipmunk blood, the murderous spit and tick of a twenty-pound grenade.

To cut. Toenails like tusks. At home, Dad clipped the kids'—eight feet in a row—over a page of newspaper during Little House on the Prairie. Then bowls of popcorn. The smell of No-Tears shampoo.

EXILE

She was sent and went.

Too hard for her to see
what must be done

with the skeleton. Hospital.
Vigilance. Isolation.

> (Easier, they said, for her
> to be likewise elsewhere, with all
> her questions and judgments,
> all her fuck yous and ruckus.)

She was sent
and now escapes

> to the cove to lie flat
> in a bashed canoe
> where she counts her ribs
> in solidarity, like a rosary.

UNTIL

The girl is not unhappy, mornings dusting
the fancy stereo listening to the Singing Nun,
the only album not in Italian. She is not unhappy
the morning she attempts a berry compote until

the Grandmother falls sloppily out of bed.

Not the weight so much as the smell. Not the smell
so much as the feel: a hundred pounds of loose person,
coughing, cursing, struggling, but not ashamed.

The Eye of the Tiger

It's the decade of the rowdy hair bands,
all their brash hardness, the beat and bellow.
The girl lets rawness barrel in at night,
her cheek pressed against the big silver boom box.

She allows herself to touch herself, to imagine
sweat and thrusting, the thrumming of *something*
that is beginning in the dark amber glow
of the radio's tiny hot On/Off light.

Tiger Lily

The Grandmother wants to see
from her bedroom window what's
leaving her, and just how far it goes,

but says instead to the college kid,
paint it so no one will steal it. He paints it,
and the girl hates it—heavy, jolting—

the bright orange row boat
the Grandmother names
after a flower. The girl takes

the canoe, a milkweed pod
that hides in dusk and fog. Hides
her drifting on the calm lake

thinking of the college kid,
his forearms flecked as if with pollen,
his collar bone glistening.

ELIZABETH

The girl never misses her sister.

Never misses her running, manic,
around the yard after supper—
mosquitoes in the wake of a scarecrow.

Never misses her retching
in the turquoise-tiled bathroom—
a wispy princess entranced by spindles.

The girl never eats

without thinking of her sister.
It makes the sweet rolls rancid
and the lamb a tough mouthful

of sadness. Still, she aims forkfuls
at her mouth and swallows. She aims
her eyes at some middle distance.

The girl never misses.

THE REFINERY

The Grandmother aims to teach the girl
something about living

in the manner of the educated, the refined.
She painfully ladles out mint jelly,

digs at whipped butter. The Grandmother
insists on chanterelles and saffron, impossible

to find on the island. The girl
pounds veal with a pocked mallet,

then attempts crème brulee, stirring
continuously while continuously

the Grandmother scolds and stabs
her Pall Mall at the preparations and utensils.

Even so, the girl fails to make the strange food
savory, succulent, smooth. She fails to forsake

Indiana with its pork rinds and potlucks.
She craves a certain sandwich—

Wonder Bread, peanut butter, marshmallow fluff.
Smudges and crumbs. Her own bed.

ORDERLY

At dawn her uncle the vegan
stops by the cottage on his way

to his own house to pillage the fridge
for leftover braised pork or crown roast.

All night at the hospital, he'd also longed
for a heaping mound of ice cream,

all the fat and sucrose, to eat it
in the almost-dark and away

from his disappointed wife.
All night the girl longs

to hear her uncle's car
chewing up the driveway,

the platter and scoop clattering,
a grown-up of sorts in the house.

THE PROFESSOR

A letter from her father.

His hand on paper. The familiar.
She skips over what it says
(the daily, the funny), focuses instead

on how he must have written it during lunch—
green olives and cream cheese between slabs
of thick-crusted bread, a lemon yogurt—
at his desk, the fountain burbling below
University Hall, his hand square, thumbnail
blacked that weekend by a fumbled hammer.

His hand jotted across the page,
just as she skims now across the lake
in the canoe holding the letter.

The square.

Shot of Morphine

The Uncle comes to take the Grandmother to the hospital. For the pain. For a shot
of morphine. First there is shouting. About the ice cream. About the negligence. The girl
has packed the Grandmother's purse full of Pall Malls and Kleenex. She's rubbed
the eyeglasses with a spritz of Windex and slicked the frayed hair into the semblance
of a head-shape. When they're gone, the girl looks at herself naked in the mirror. She is
not injured. She is, in her way, a bit beautiful.

BELONGINGS

When they were sisters

the girl and her sister played for days
in the old blue house in Silver Spring
while their mother packed the Grandmother's
belongings in Bekins boxes for the move
up north. The sisters ransacked the attic,
the basement, the barn. They dressed up
in musty hats and laughed. When they
were sisters, they ate Nilla Wafers on the porch
with huge sycamore leaves beneath their feet
to keep cool. Now they're apart.

They're not sisters but two bodies, apart.

One feasts on solitude and lake water,
the other trapped, in-patient, by a room
in Indiana, feasts on herself. This summer,
they never talk, never write. If one dreams
of the attic, there's some other girl there,
a ghost in a funny hat.

Trapper Keeper

The girl will have to change herself to return,
she knows this, understands

that her friends will not understand
the canoe and the morphine. She will be
an 8th grader, and must wear pretty clothes,
speak in a way that reveals nothing
but giddy concern for skating parties.

She will have to convince her mother to purchase
the proper binders, backpack, back-pocket comb.
The girl will have to change her smell
of Griselda,
of cigarettes,
of Bon Ami.

The girl understands this: if she has changed,
she must change again.

Awake

And when the news turns in alarm to a tourist in the National Park who found a wad
of flesh on the beach, a human tongue cut free and lapping the cold salt and sand, the girl
closes her mouth. A black-redness opens inside her, then overcomes her. She is awake.
Loons shriek and chortle all night on the lake. Bouncing lightly, the canoe makes
a lullaby against the dock. But the girl is awake with the bloody darkness. A letter
is writing itself on the red coverlet: *Come get me.*

Come Get Me

She starts a letter to her father. She will craft this letter many times
over many years. Come get me. Come help me unravel the sadness.

I'm alone in the woods with a woman who could burn down
the house and the cat and your daughter in one drunken instance

of listening to Pavarotti, smoking, while dreaming of Cyprus. Come.
Save me too from the lunatic who chops tongues from shouting mouths.

Come get me in our old green, stripped-down van with a plastic tub
full of celery and carrots, sacks of Fig Newtons, tins of lunch meat.

I won't complain about the AM radio. Won't beg to stop at a hotel
with a pool. I love you. I'll read the Road Atlas and sing country.

Come get me. I'll be good and not say a word about the scarecrow
in the hospital. Won't pitch fits for you and Mom to bring her home.

Only come get me—the girl who looks like you, and your mother.
Not her mother. Not the woman who could burn me down and shrug.

BROOMSTICK

A witch
        pokes her broomstick
from inside
        the girl's chest. It makes
hard spots
        of tenderness. Raspberries
ripen in the garden,
        and the girl picks them
for dessert.

A witch sits
        at the table, complaining
the mascarpone
        is too runny. The girl
shuts her eyes,
        sees splinters of light
refracting
        inside her chest, which is now
a basket,
        a thin woven thing to be carried.

Church, Drunk

The Grandmother takes off
for church, drunk. The girl,
who will not get in the car,
locks herself in the bathroom.

Shortly, the police come and want
to speak to the responsible party.

They phone the Uncle, next
the girl's mother who agrees
with everything: license/suspension,
hospital/observation.

Then there is nothing more
to be done.

The girl sits on the dock.
Closes her mouth.

Rum Island

In the canoe, the girl reads a book
about a young wife who lived in a castle,
terrified by the housekeeper and an idea

of the first wife. Eagles circle overhead,
and the girl dips her hand into a sack
of apricots. The young wife was wrong

and was deceived, but all the while,
loved. It's not enough to think, the girl
thinks. *I must see and feel.* She begins

to paddle. Ahead is an island
with the charred remains of a shack.
She spends the day there on the rocks

amid wintergreen and crayfish. She makes
no sound. Her skin browns. The girl trusts
the sun not to burn her. She has an idea

to return before dark, but does not.
Because no one needs her tonight,
she stays, watches, breathes, eats fruit.

CURSE

What to put on   or in,

      cotton balls?
      dish towels?

          The girl settles   on guest napkins,

crams them
in her
pants.

Soft enough   swath of alyssum
          feather of egret

and not marked
      with the family's   subtle monogram   creamy beige

          elegant

but quickly and brightly   with blood   like a bark of surprise

          then pain.

AXE

Beyond the laundry machines,
past the shelves of paint cans
and toxic solvents, the axe

juts up from an old stump
in the basement. When she dreams
of a monster coming, smothering her,

then chopping out her tongue
with the axe, she figures it's herself
hurting herself. This notion calms her,

saves her, stays with her. She lobs a sandal
when Griselda slinks up the cool steps,
glares into the girl's room, and growls.

FAITH

The Grandmother was a doctor entrusted
with the research of complicated cancers.
She clipped off to work in her white coat and pumps
to ferret out errant cells. In addition, she studied

Greek and Hebrew, the monetary systems
of Africa. Well-travelled, a woman of faith,
of four children who begged to please her.
Her son then husband died, and she crept off

to Maine with her drink and smokes and recollections
of the white coat, the exotic lands that fill her dreams
from which she rises now in agony in all her joints,
her mind, and if there is a soul . . .

she drinks and dozes and smokes.

FRIEND

The girl sneaks a cigarette and does not
hate it

or cough up her guts as she's heard of
but feels

a tingle of relief
and ease,

a dangerous alliance
with need.

Her thick hair smells of it,
the savory secret,

the private self pulling
at mist

with the island blurring
all around.

It will follow her
like a cat, quietly,

quietly—this sneaky
promise

of some release
from grief.

Meanwhile

Always meanwhile:

the sister she loves, dying,
or else just lying about the last meal
she took in. *Robust, flavorful, substantial!*

The blue-starred gown floats
like the universe around her legs.
The pegs. The pale replicas. Daily,

the weigh-in displays some slight
improvement. But it's only water
sucked down before mounting

the scale. The smaller girl
is now larger, the larger girl,
a desiccated stump in the basement
in which an axe tilts and perplexes

the sister who loves her,
who in dreams can almost reach
the worn and glossy handle,
yank the blade out.

Awake

The girl is old. She does not sleep. She strains her eyes into the shifting pines. Someone is coming. She knows the axe waits in the basement, and fillet knives hang on the kitchen's magnet. What if she must leap forward to save herself? She does not wish to leap forward. She wishes to be small again in her small town where her father jogged down the snowy street dragging a toboggan, his girls hooting in a spray of ice. It's hot on the island tonight. Someone is coming.

THE APPRENTICE

She learned many good things—fine cooking,
gentle care of the infirm, resilience in the face

of nightmares. And lastingly, the solace of language,
water, and quiet. You'd be right to presume strength

in these. But the girl's greatest lesson was to be afraid
of being afraid. And this has proven to be not at all useful.

APART

The Grandmother will die, and the girl's mother
will fall

to the floor of the Indiana kitchen, never quite
to rise.

The girl will view this not in horror but from
apart.

> A shack burned on an island.
> A canoe bashed itself on the dock.
> A stereo boomed at midnight.
> A soufflé refused to rise.

A woman falls to the floor. It's been done
before.

The girl would like to lift up, to comfort.
She'd like

to go back and sew the holes shut,
to laugh off

the tongue as a dime store mystery.
She'd like

a bowl of nectarines. Dragonflies.
Sleep.

Awake

Of course it turns out
the tongue was just

a slice of sea cucumber.

That it took so long
for the experts to discern this

is ridiculous, and the girl

is suspicious. She believes
it's a lie so the island

may now be over-run
with placated vacationers.

She believes in the tongue.

That someone is coming
to take hers. But now she will

not allow it. She has constructed
all her barricades:

words, smoke, silence. Her safety.
The girl returns to Indiana awake.

Vigilant. Tough as a stump.

Or maybe she never leaves. Never turns thirteen. The girl is still
on the island, in the cottage, on her hands and knees, cleaning. Still hiding
from the baleful cat, scared of an axe. Maybe the girl stays put
but doesn't mind, and her sister stays thin but doesn't die. They stay,
and their staying goes on and on.

Hollow

Requiem

We went to church for the concerts in matching dresses, grubbing in pigeonholes
for stubby pencils to play tic-tac-toe before the conductor raised his dry-spaghetti baton.

Oh, the thrill of the singers filing in, spotting our mother among them, a slim black book
with red lipstick. Only my sister could read. She traced the program with her finger,

inching us closer to Intermission, then after, the sweet frenzy of the Reception.
We always ended up prostrate on the pew by the encore, no longer clapping, no longer

trying in vain to make our mother wave. Years later, when she slid into a U-Haul, I too
refused to wave. I heard a thump and rumble and no more. All those concerts, I'd slept

with my head on my sister's leg. Through all of it—fabric, flesh, bone, wood, the dozens
of voices—I thought I could hear my mother. I always thought I could.

HOLLOW

By leaving, our mother cured us.

Like sides of beef hanging
in a hollow tree, she cured us.

Smoke and cold and time.

The rusted hooks.

GRAND

Our anger is a piano—black, massive—standing
in the center of a thickly frozen lake, its music

dormant. The awful silence bludgeons
everything: the pines, the barns, the towns

which hunker low and hastily close over
with snow. Nothing dares move except below

in the sludgy light through a foot of ice
a few homely catfish—our sadness—insensibly twitch.

COROLLA

She taught me to drive
by screaming and slapping me
as I clutched the wheel,
shifting wildly, careening
through the countryside
where tall corn hid
oncoming pickups.
I blew through stop signs,
turned on two wheels.
My sister screamed.   We
never died. Instead we saw
a boy bare-chested on a tractor
standing up in the sun. We
wanted to water him, slap him,
trap him in a pen. Stars
in our own soft-core stories,
we concocted notions
of abandoned farmhouses,
claw-foot bathtubs. Later,
when the boy took me
to a dance, I came home
to report how he grabbed
my breast like a piglet,
his breath in my face all
Swisher Sweet and Pemmican.

And my sister stiffened, drifted
away. Better she had slapped me.

HUNGER FOR SOMETHING EASIER

I suppose now you'll deny it all:
there was no wild pig in the woods,
hair up on his back like barbed wire,
eyes sunk and runny in crusted tunnels
along the snout. And we didn't run
through red brambles, banging our legs
against stumps until we flung ourselves
into the thorny arms of an apple tree.
You'll say we didn't stay shoved up
against the bark breathing bright spice
and pitching green fruit to frighten away
the pig. You'll never say you were afraid
or that I held you and you held me
and we crouched on the thin branches
until night slunk in, and a hunger
for something easier turned the pig away.

STILL

There's the field where an errant sunflower towers,
and there's the boy running to snag this huge happiness.

The car is a red oval on the road, wide open as a heart
before misfortune. The girl sits with the flower in her lap,

its hundred eyelids fuzzed, placid. They drive flat west
through heat full of pollen and barn swallows, and the boy

is good with his clean hair and steady eyes and knows nothing.

At home the girl finds a bucket
and drowns the sunflower in it.

All that bright cheery softness.

Because her house is silent
in its dry rot, its open socket.

Because her mother is gone.

Food, music, the click of rings, gone.

And because none of it returns even
as summer dumps out its fullness

like ridiculous, over-much love

all around town. Loads of corn,
of kittens, weeds, locusts . . .

It hurts and empties her.

And the girl begins to believe
that terrible things are certain to happen.

She'd imagined herself opening
the car door while the boy was driving,

seen herself falling and turning
into blood and glass and asphalt.

✱

He was a house in a field. He slept against me and never left me.

✱

She wraps his ring, silver/amethyst,
in thick yarn and acts normal. But
she's becoming clothes and hair,
a barrel of ash. In her empty house
a raccoon creeps in, spitting whiteness.
The boy comes with a net and bat,
but too late. The girl has already knelt
before the animal and breathed its anger
like smoke. She laughs at the boy.
He goes away, betrayed. She sleeps.

And in her dream, black claws, delicate
and cruel, tear at her night shirt.

✱

In dreams, he carries me up the stairs of an old white house adrift
in snow and wheat. It is February but also August. The light
in the house is so clear and pale it tastes of frozen pears.

The boy works nights at a hotel
off the highway behind a plastic window
the thickness of the girl's diary.

She writes pages of words:

I am waiting
for the sun to roll
through me

then walks deep into the field
and sits down.

To calm herself, she imagines
that she is the boy.

She begins to press
the bones of her face
the bones that are
her face. She eats
nothing, but craves
cheese and pasta
and the silence
of a steak on a plate
to escape into smoke
across a long yard
where owls can see
her small movements.
Then she'd be
the steak on the plate
a pellet of bones
and fur. The boy

will not allow it.
He feeds her bits
of meat from his hand.
She begins to hate
his hands and the way
he kisses the edges
of her eyes.

I live as if he still loves me, and therefore cannot say my life
dismays me. Once he took three oranges from a wooden bowl
and began juggling. I live still surprised by this. I still
remember exactly the shape of his hands. The sound
of oranges rising and descending.

The girl loses sense
of years. She sleeps
on the boy's floor
next to the couch.

When she wakes, she's older and growing
an illness like ferns —all fists and shyness.

The boy still
smells of soap
and mown fields,
still feeds her.

They take the red car to a house on a hill off the road to school.
And this is how it ends. His sturdy body. The empty house.

My Father's Face

There wasn't enough
and nothing else to be done.

Blonde chunks of sun
crashed around me all summer—

you won't be going, won't be

the bad news found me
at the creek, in the fields, working

in a nursing home where I marked charts,
row after row of not-yet-dead.

Yes, the cake was delicately iced
in red. I learned all the songs

and coughed them up. I learned
there wouldn't be enough.

For a long while I sat looking at my hands
as if they were dead birds.

Then I pulled my father's face
over my own and walked into the world.

Slice of Glass

Because it was decided upon.
Because yarrow took over the yard.
Because I slept on the porch and woke
to a squirrel clutching the screen,

its bright throat a wedge of rage.
Because the road opened like a storm,
and sorrow slapped me in the coal room.

Rats cavorted in the hay mow,
mold bloomed like luxury.

Because the sun was arrogant in the graveyard,
the bowl of fruit a skull in my lap,
the taste of one raspberry a shiver of death.

Because cows lowed in the toxic creek.
Because the bull's-eye window winked.

And the road opened like a storm.
There was nothing left but a slice of glass
clinging to the window's strict frame.
Because that glass . . . I decided.

I left that house.

I left that house
and now stand wanting it in another.

My Anxious Whisper is a Form of Fierce Sweetness
—George Kalamaras, *Pray the Blind Syllable*

This is the final day of years of sweetness.
And now I lay me down. In a grove rimmed
in wild raspberries. A man with constellations

of freckles on his shoulders runs a small gold
Matchbox car along my hips and ribs.
It's noon, July. Whosoever calls upon him

shall bow down. In the sun, in the raw scent
of berries and sorghum. Above, a crow watches.
I want to be watched, then forgotten. Not

to pray, lazy with sex and heat. Still, I pray
to a God I've imagined all these years
as a small gold car, a bit of glint and spin.

Forgive Us Our Trespass

The sun is a smear of stained glass.

The cut below my belly makes me mortal
and morbid, blurred in the aftermath.

Prayerful. What I see is my torso
scored deeply by Fernalds' creek bed

where my mother and sister gathered watercress
with quick hands into muddy baskets.

A toddler, I drifted to fiddling
with crawdads, blurred by heat and sleepiness.

When the mutt raced toward me,
let loose from its chain on the hill,

I blinked, vaguely amazed, and was devoured.

SMALL GRAY HOUSE
for Grace

Once upon a time there was a girl
who began in a red brick house in a small town.

She *was* the town, in her little darkness, as she lay in the creek,
in shallow water, and became water. She curled in the arms

of a hedge apple tree and grew into that tree. After a time,
the girl never went home. The red house frightened her

with its furious air. And yet she always watched the house
from the woods, safe in the shaggy limbs of the tree.

She crept out to eat from cat dishes crusted over in the barn
and soon became a round-backed raccoon. Her brothers

pitched gravel at her in the dusk, in the wafting clouds
of mosquito mist, then gaped and chased her,

returning to the red house with implausible tales
of a scavenger wearing their sister's face.

Now there is another girl who lives
in a small gray house in another town.

She loves her mother so fiercely it makes them both
afraid of dying. She often wakes to a shadow in her room,

a smoky black curve darting backwards.
The girl cries until her mother's face rises pale

at her bedside, and the night falls away. The night
flows aside like water, like the warmth of rich earth,

before it comes back. By then the girl is asleep, curled
around the tough gray creature who never leaves.

INDELIBLE

The pen, uncapped,
leaves a rough-edged patch

of wet red
on our fancy sheets.

One of us says
Beach rose

The other,
Exit wound.

ADORATION

We're so careful with each other,
even out here in the driveway
where we're the grown-ups,
playing with our daughters—

water balloons, chalk on the asphalt.
When I trace my sister's body
I make sure to draw the lines smooth
and narrow, the waist nipped in.

She decorates the outline of me
with exotic clothes, lush hair,
and says *Of course you're beautiful.*
We make our lovely dusty selves

hold hands, grind pink slashes
into huge smiles, big thought bubbles
proclaim *I adore you.*
But nonetheless our drawings,

so difficult, so generous, so fabulous,
look like fancy homicides.
And that night the rain sweeps in,
rinses us blessedly away.

COYDOG
for Noah

When I look at you
my life, my eyes
grow lighter, become
a golden coydog's.

I cannot touch you
enough and already
have learned not to try
to trap or tame you,

not even to untangle
your hair. It is enough
that the look of you
lightens me

until I could run
the fields behind our house,
twisting and yipping
with joy.

WIDE OPEN

Our Dad said he would, and he did:
mounted the stairs, toolbox banging,

and calmly removed the bedroom door.
My sister the door-slammer slept a week

wide open to the hall. Our Dad said
he would. Years later, he cradled

her child who was failing, suffering,
and stole away to the basement.

To not hear a prognosis. To not see
his daughter's face pale as tallow.

Or perhaps to show the baby
the workroom: here are wrenches

and files and screwdrivers. Long rows
of solid things that take apart and fix.

Pediatric Surgery

We must love this world, though it is flawed,
must love it entirely, or be lost. I loved my sister

the day she came home from first grade waving
a picture of me, my arms wobbling out

from my skull, my stick-legs jutting from my chin.
All my life, I have loved her and feared her,

like all good pets. And yet. Though I have no body,
no torso containing a gut and heart, I sit here with her.

Here, in the waiting room, while her child
is pried apart, I sit and talk and talk.

PULLING IT OFF

Once again I've worn my name tag for hours
in public—all evening, in fact—after the conference.

I've been so happy. All the slow, kind smiles as though
I'm mildly famous or beloved, at least memorable.

The bag boy and dry cleaner thank me personally,
and I glow with the small-townness of Chicago.

Then again, I fake nearly everything. For years
in waking dreams, I've pictured a henchman

in a trench coat approaching, jabbing his finger
as I elbow my way to the office in knock-off shoes.

Faker. Fraud. Do- and Know-nothing! he hisses,
and the faceless forms of those diligently trying,

remarkably earnest, part in disgust on the sidewalk,
then tsk tsk me to death in the Loop. Death,

in my knock-off shoes. Once again, I've worn
out my welcome. Snake oil, shell games.

My name on the tag is misspelled. Also backwards
in the wavy mirror back home. And I believe

I may be sick, inspecting something bashed
and abashed in the spit-freckled glass. I believe

I may be myself: no one's quirky darling,
no one's lost daughter, no one's first love.

THE CHILD

Geese blacken
        the sky above
our house
        where my son finally
sleeps
        in his nest-bed
smelling
        of bile and sweat.

I also stink
        but of aloneness.
It's early morning
        and cold.

The birds cry
        Ma Ma Ma!
And I can't tell
        if the call
comes for me
        or from me.

QUEEN ANNE'S LACE

Lowered into the mountains, the mountains
lowered into me. I ran on the dirt road until
I became flowers. I found my way with a pointed stick,
pointing it at the brown dog with the shriveled leg
that shadowed me. I found a plain house with beige rooms
and ate off a cutting board with a plastic fork.

You know how it is. You must live.

Biographical Note

Rachel Contreni Flynn's second full-length collection, *Tongue*, won the Benjamin Saltman Award and was published by Red Hen Press in 2010. A chapbook, *Haywire*, was published by Bright Hill Press in 2009, and her first book, *Ice, Mouth, Song*, was published in 2005 by Tupelo Press after winning the Dorset Prize. She was awarded a Fellowship from the National Endowment for the Arts in 2007. Her work has often been nominated for Pushcart Prizes, and she received an Illinois Arts Council Artists Fellowship in 2003. She received her MFA from Warren Wilson College in 2001 and lives north of Chicago with her husband and their two children.